Meals She Eats

Meals She Eats

Lila Thompson

CONTENTS █

Introduction

Welcome Message

Welcome to "Meals She Eats: A PCOS Cookbook for Insulin Resistance Diet, Hormone Balance, and Period Repair Manual." This cookbook is more than just a collection of recipes; it's a heartfelt guide to navigating the challenges of PCOS with delicious, nourishing meals that support your health and well-being.

I remember the day I was diagnosed with PCOS like it was yesterday. The mix of emotions—fear, confusion, and a sense of helplessness—was overwhelming. The doctor's words were a blur, but one thing stood out: the importance of diet in managing my symptoms. That day marked the beginning of my journey to understand and combat PCOS, not just for myself, but for countless women who share this struggle.

This cookbook is born out of my personal journey and the countless hours spent researching, experimenting, and refining recipes that not only taste great but also help manage PCOS symptoms. I want to share with you the knowledge I've gained and the meals that have brought balance and joy back into my life. My hope is that these recipes will become staples in your kitchen, offering you comfort, health, and a sense of empowerment.

Understanding PCOS

Polycystic Ovary Syndrome (PCOS) is a common hormonal disorder affecting millions of women worldwide. It's characterized by symptoms such as irregular menstrual cycles, excess hair growth, acne, and, often, insulin resistance. These symptoms can vary greatly from one woman to another, making PCOS a complex and often frustrating condition to manage.

For many women, one of the biggest challenges of PCOS is dealing with insulin resistance, a condition where the body's cells become less responsive to insulin, leading to higher blood sugar levels. This can result in weight gain, increased hunger, and a higher risk of developing type 2 diabetes. Managing insulin resistance through diet is crucial for alleviating many of the symptoms associated with PCOS.

Diet plays a pivotal role in managing PCOS. A balanced diet can help regulate blood sugar levels, reduce inflammation, and support hormone balance. This cookbook focuses on meals that are rich in fiber, lean proteins, and healthy fats, while minimizing refined sugars and carbohydrates. These recipes are designed to help you maintain stable blood sugar levels, support hormone health, and provide the necessary nutrients your body needs.

Insulin Resistance and Hormone Balance

Insulin resistance is a common issue for many women with PCOS. When the body becomes resistant to insulin, it produces more of it to try to keep blood sugar levels in check. This excess insulin can cause the ovaries to produce more androgens (male hormones), which can exacerbate PCOS symptoms like irregular periods, acne, and hair growth.

Balancing hormones is essential for managing PCOS, and diet is a powerful tool in achieving this balance. Foods that are high in fiber and protein can help regulate blood sugar levels and reduce insulin spikes. Healthy fats, such as those found in avocados, nuts, and olive oil, are crucial for hormone production and overall health.

Real-life example: One of the recipes you'll find in this cookbook is a Quinoa and Black Bean Salad. Quinoa is a high-fiber grain that helps stabilize blood sugar levels, while black beans provide a good source of protein. Combined with a variety of colorful vegetables and a zesty lime dressing, this salad is not only delicious but also supports your body's insulin and hormone balance.

How to Use This Cookbook

Navigating this cookbook is simple and intuitive. Each chapter is dedicated to a different type of meal, from breakfast to dinner, snacks to desserts, and even beverages. You'll find recipes that are easy to prepare, with ingredients that are both accessible and nutritious.

Here are a few tips to help you get the most out of this cookbook:

1. **Meal Planning**: Start by planning your meals for the week. This will help you stay organized, make grocery shopping easier, and ensure you have all the ingredients you need on hand.

2. **Preparation**: Many of the recipes in this cookbook can be prepared ahead of time. Consider batch cooking on weekends so you have healthy, PCOS-friendly meals ready to go during the busy week.

3. **Stay Motivated**: Managing PCOS through diet is a journey. Celebrate your successes, no matter how small, and don't be too hard on yourself if you slip up. Every meal is an opportunity to nourish your body and support your health.

Remember, this cookbook is more than just recipes—it's a companion on your journey to better health. The stories, tips, and personal insights shared throughout are meant to inspire and support you every step of the way. Enjoy the process, and savor the delicious meals that will help you feel your best.

Breakfast Boosters

Breakfast is often called the most important meal of the day, and for women with PCOS, it truly can be. A nutritious breakfast sets the tone for the rest of your day, helping to stabilize blood sugar levels, curb cravings, and provide sustained energy. Starting your day with a balanced meal can significantly impact how you feel and function throughout the day.

When I was first diagnosed with PCOS, breakfast became a cornerstone of my routine. I discovered that skipping breakfast or eating something high in sugar and low in nutrients would lead to a rollercoaster of energy crashes and cravings later in the day. Through trial and error, I found that a breakfast rich in protein, healthy fats, and fiber helped me feel full, energized, and ready to take on the day.

In this chapter, you'll find a collection of breakfast recipes that are not only delicious but also specifically designed to support hormone balance and manage insulin resistance. From smoothie bowls packed with antioxidants to hearty egg muffins loaded with veggies, these recipes will make your mornings something to look forward to.

Hormone-Balancing Smoothie Bowls

Servings: 2 | *Prep Time:* 10 mins | *Cook Time:* 0 mins
Ingredients:

- 1 cup spinach
- 1 cup frozen mixed berries
- 1 banana
- 1 cup almond milk
- 1 tablespoon chia seeds
- 1 tablespoon almond butter
- 1 teaspoon maca powder

Instructions:

1. In a blender, combine spinach, frozen berries, banana, and almond milk. Blend until smooth.
2. Add chia seeds, almond butter, and maca powder. Blend again until well combined.
3. Pour into bowls and top with your favorite toppings such as fresh fruit, nuts, and seeds.

Nutritional Information:

- Calories: 250
- Protein: 8g
- Carbs: 35g
- Fat: 12g

Cooking Tips:

- Freeze the banana beforehand for an even creamier texture.
- Add a scoop of protein powder for an extra protein boost.

Allergen Information:

- Contains nuts (almond butter). Substitute with sunflower seed butter if needed.

Insulin-Resistant-Friendly Oatmeal

Servings: 2 | *Prep Time:* 5 mins | *Cook Time:* 10 mins
Ingredients:

- 1 cup rolled oats
- 2 cups water or almond milk
- 1 teaspoon cinnamon
- 1 tablespoon ground flaxseed
- 1/2 cup fresh berries
- 1 tablespoon almond butter

Instructions:

1. In a saucepan, bring water or almond milk to a boil. Add rolled oats and reduce heat to a simmer.
2. Cook oats for about 5-7 minutes, stirring occasionally, until they reach your desired consistency.
3. Stir in cinnamon and ground flaxseed.
4. Divide oatmeal into bowls and top with fresh berries and a dollop of almond butter.

Nutritional Information:

- Calories: 300
- Protein: 10g
- Carbs: 45g
- Fat: 10g

Cooking Tips:

- Prepare overnight oats by soaking the ingredients in a jar overnight for a quick, no-cook option.
- Mix in some Greek yogurt for added creaminess and protein.

Allergen Information:

- Contains nuts (almond butter). Substitute with sunflower seed butter if needed.

Egg Muffins with Veggies

Servings: 6 | _Prep Time:_ 15 mins | _Cook Time:_ 20 mins
Ingredients:

- 6 large eggs
- 1/4 cup almond milk
- 1 cup chopped spinach
- 1/2 cup diced bell peppers
- 1/4 cup chopped onions
- Salt and pepper to taste
- 1/4 cup shredded cheese (optional)

Instructions:

1. Preheat oven to 350°F (175°C). Grease a muffin tin or line with silicone muffin cups.
2. In a large bowl, whisk together eggs and almond milk.
3. Stir in spinach, bell peppers, onions, salt, and pepper.
4. Pour the egg mixture evenly into the muffin tin cups. Top with shredded cheese if using.
5. Bake for 20-25 minutes, or until the egg muffins are set and lightly golden.

Nutritional Information:

- Calories: 100 (without cheese)
- Protein: 8g
- Carbs: 3g
- Fat: 6g

Cooking Tips:

- These muffins can be stored in the refrigerator for up to 5 days or frozen for longer storage.
- Customize with your favorite veggies and spices.

Allergen Information:

- Contains eggs and dairy (if using cheese). Omit cheese for a dairy-free option.

Greek Yogurt Parfaits with Berries and Nuts

Servings: 2 | _Prep Time:_ 5 mins | _Cook Time:_ 0 mins
Ingredients:

- 1 cup Greek yogurt
- 1/2 cup mixed berries (strawberries, blueberries, raspberries)
- 1/4 cup granola
- 2 tablespoons chopped nuts (almonds, walnuts)
- 1 tablespoon honey (optional)

Instructions:

1. In two serving glasses or bowls, layer Greek yogurt, mixed berries, granola, and chopped nuts.
2. Drizzle with honey if desired.

Nutritional Information:

- Calories: 250
- Protein: 12g
- Carbs: 30g
- Fat: 10g

Cooking Tips:

- Use plain Greek yogurt to avoid added sugars.
- Substitute granola with chia seeds or flaxseeds for a lower-carb option.

Allergen Information:

- Contains nuts. Omit or substitute with seeds if needed.

Avocado and Smoked Salmon Toast

Servings: 2 | *Prep Time:* 10 mins | *Cook Time:* 0 mins
Ingredients:

- 2 slices whole-grain bread
- 1 ripe avocado
- 4 oz smoked salmon
- 1 tablespoon lemon juice
- Salt and pepper to taste
- Optional: red pepper flakes, capers

Instructions:

1. Toast the whole-grain bread slices to your liking.
2. In a small bowl, mash the avocado with lemon juice, salt, and pepper.
3. Spread the mashed avocado evenly on each slice of toast.
4. Top with smoked salmon and optional toppings like red pepper flakes or capers.

Nutritional Information:

- Calories: 350
- Protein: 15g
- Carbs: 25g
- Fat: 22g

Cooking Tips:

- For added fiber, use sprouted grain bread.
- Drizzle with a bit of olive oil for extra healthy fats.

Allergen Information:

- Contains fish (smoked salmon).

3

Nourishing Lunches

Lunch is a critical meal for maintaining energy levels and hormone balance throughout the day. For women with PCOS, a balanced lunch can help prevent afternoon energy crashes and curb cravings, supporting steady blood sugar levels. I vividly remember my struggles with lunch in the early days of managing my PCOS. Often, I'd reach for quick, carb-heavy options that left me feeling sluggish and irritable. It wasn't until I started prioritizing nutrient-dense, balanced meals that I noticed a significant improvement in my energy and overall well-being.

In this chapter, you'll find lunch recipes that are not only nutritious but also easy to prepare. These meals are designed to be quick enough for a busy day while providing the necessary nutrients to keep you feeling satisfied and energized. From hearty salads to flavorful wraps, these recipes will make your lunchtime both enjoyable and beneficial for your health.

Quinoa and Black Bean Salad

Servings: 4 | *Prep Time:* 15 mins | *Cook Time:* 15 mins
Ingredients:

- 1 cup quinoa
- 2 cups water
- 1 can (15 oz) black beans, drained and rinsed
- 1 cup cherry tomatoes, halved
- 1 cup corn kernels (fresh or frozen)
- 1 red bell pepper, diced
- 1/4 cup red onion, finely chopped
- 1/4 cup fresh cilantro, chopped
- Juice of 2 limes
- 2 tablespoons olive oil
- Salt and pepper to taste

Instructions:

1. Rinse quinoa under cold water. In a medium saucepan, bring water to a boil. Add quinoa, reduce heat, cover, and simmer for 15 minutes or until water is absorbed. Fluff with a fork and let cool.
2. In a large bowl, combine cooked quinoa, black beans, cherry tomatoes, corn, bell pepper, red onion, and cilantro.
3. In a small bowl, whisk together lime juice, olive oil, salt, and pepper. Pour over salad and toss to coat.

Nutritional Information:

- Calories: 220
- Protein: 8g
- Carbs: 38g
- Fat: 6g

Cooking Tips:

- Make this salad ahead of time and let it chill in the refrigerator for the flavors to meld.
- Add diced avocado for extra creaminess and healthy fats.

Allergen Information:

- None. Ensure all ingredients are gluten-free if you have gluten sensitivities.

Grilled Chicken and Veggie Wraps

Servings: 4 | *Prep Time:* 20 mins | *Cook Time:* 10 mins
Ingredients:

- 2 boneless, skinless chicken breasts
- 2 tablespoons olive oil
- 1 teaspoon garlic powder
- 1 teaspoon paprika
- Salt and pepper to taste
- 4 whole-grain tortillas
- 1 cup mixed greens
- 1/2 cup shredded carrots
- 1/2 cup diced cucumber
- 1/2 cup hummus

Instructions:

1. Preheat grill to medium-high heat. Brush chicken breasts with olive oil and season with garlic powder, paprika, salt, and pepper.
2. Grill chicken for 5-7 minutes on each side or until fully cooked. Let rest for 5 minutes, then slice thinly.
3. To assemble wraps, spread hummus on each tortilla. Layer with mixed greens, shredded carrots, cucumber, and grilled chicken slices. Roll up tightly and slice in half.

Nutritional Information:

- Calories: 350
- Protein: 25g
- Carbs: 30g
- Fat: 15g

Cooking Tips:

- Use leftover grilled chicken for a quick and easy lunch.
- Add your favorite veggies or switch up the greens for variety.

Allergen Information:

- Contains gluten (whole-grain tortillas). Use gluten-free tortillas if needed.

Lentil and Spinach Soup

Servings: 6 | *Prep Time:* 10 mins | *Cook Time:* 30 mins
Ingredients:

- 1 tablespoon olive oil
- 1 onion, diced
- 2 cloves garlic, minced
- 2 carrots, diced
- 2 celery stalks, diced
- 1 cup dried lentils, rinsed
- 6 cups vegetable broth
- 1 can (14.5 oz) diced tomatoes
- 1 teaspoon cumin
- 1 teaspoon turmeric
- Salt and pepper to taste
- 4 cups fresh spinach
- Juice of 1 lemon

Instructions:

1. In a large pot, heat olive oil over medium heat. Add onion, garlic, carrots, and celery. Sauté for 5-7 minutes until vegetables are tender.
2. Stir in lentils, vegetable broth, diced tomatoes, cumin, turmeric, salt, and pepper. Bring to a boil, then reduce heat and simmer for 20-25 minutes until lentils are tender.
3. Stir in spinach and cook for an additional 2-3 minutes until wilted. Remove from heat and stir in lemon juice.

Nutritional Information:

- Calories: 200
- Protein: 12g
- Carbs: 32g
- Fat: 4g

Cooking Tips:

- This soup freezes well. Make a big batch and freeze in individual portions for a quick lunch.
- Add a pinch of red pepper flakes for a bit of heat.

Allergen Information:

- None. Ensure vegetable broth is gluten-free if you have gluten sensitivities.

Tuna and Avocado Salad

Servings: 2 | *Prep Time:* 10 mins | *Cook Time:* 0 mins
Ingredients:

- 1 can (5 oz) tuna packed in water, drained
- 1 ripe avocado, diced
- 1/4 cup red onion, finely chopped
- 1 celery stalk, diced
- Juice of 1 lime
- Salt and pepper to taste
- 2 cups mixed greens

Instructions:

1. In a medium bowl, combine tuna, avocado, red onion, celery, lime juice, salt, and pepper. Mix gently to combine.
2. Serve over mixed greens.

Nutritional Information:

- Calories: 300
- Protein: 25g
- Carbs: 12g
- Fat: 18g

Cooking Tips:

- Use canned salmon or chicken if you prefer.
- Add a tablespoon of Greek yogurt for extra creaminess.

Allergen Information:

- Contains fish (tuna).

Zucchini Noodles with Pesto and Cherry Tomatoes

Servings: 4 | *Prep Time:* 15 mins | *Cook Time:* 5 mins
Ingredients:

- 4 medium zucchinis, spiralized
- 1 tablespoon olive oil
- 2 cups cherry tomatoes, halved
- 1/4 cup pesto (store-bought or homemade)
- Salt and pepper to taste
- Grated Parmesan cheese (optional)

Instructions:

1. Heat olive oil in a large skillet over medium heat. Add zucchini noodles and sauté for 2-3 minutes until just tender.
2. Add cherry tomatoes and cook for another 2 minutes until tomatoes are slightly softened.
3. Remove from heat and toss with pesto. Season with salt and pepper.
4. Serve with grated Parmesan cheese if desired.

Nutritional Information:

- Calories: 150
- Protein: 4g
- Carbs: 12g
- Fat: 10g

Cooking Tips:

- For a more filling meal, add grilled chicken or shrimp.
- Make your own pesto with fresh basil, pine nuts, Parmesan, garlic, and olive oil.

Allergen Information:

- Contains nuts (if using homemade pesto with pine nuts). Use nut-free pesto if needed.

4

Satisfying Dinners

Dinner plays a crucial role in maintaining hormone balance and ensuring a restful night's sleep. A well-balanced dinner can help stabilize blood sugar levels overnight, reducing the likelihood of insulin spikes that can disrupt sleep and exacerbate PCOS symptoms. During my journey with PCOS, I found that the right dinner choices made a significant difference in how I felt the next day.

Creating satisfying and nutritious dinners doesn't have to be complicated. With a bit of planning and the right recipes, you can enjoy meals that are both delicious and beneficial for your health. In this chapter, you'll find a collection of dinner recipes that are easy to prepare, full of flavor, and designed to support your body's needs.

Baked Salmon with Asparagus

Servings: 4 | _Prep Time:_ 10 mins | _Cook Time:_ 20 mins
Ingredients:

- 4 salmon fillets
- 1 bunch asparagus, trimmed
- 2 tablespoons olive oil
- 1 lemon, sliced
- 2 cloves garlic, minced
- Salt and pepper to taste
- Fresh dill for garnish (optional)

Instructions:

1. Preheat oven to 400°F (200°C). Line a baking sheet with parchment paper.
2. Place salmon fillets and asparagus on the baking sheet. Drizzle with olive oil and season with salt, pepper, and minced garlic.
3. Arrange lemon slices over the salmon and asparagus.
4. Bake for 18-20 minutes, or until salmon is cooked through and flakes easily with a fork.
5. Garnish with fresh dill if desired and serve immediately.

Nutritional Information:

- Calories: 350
- Protein: 30g
- Carbs: 6g
- Fat: 22g

Cooking Tips:

- Use wild-caught salmon for the best flavor and nutritional benefits.
- Add a sprinkle of Parmesan cheese on the asparagus for extra flavor.

Allergen Information:

- Contains fish (salmon).

Chicken Stir-Fry with Broccoli and Bell Peppers

Servings: 4 | *Prep Time:* 15 mins | *Cook Time:* 15 mins
Ingredients:

- 2 tablespoons olive oil
- 1 pound boneless, skinless chicken breasts, sliced thinly
- 2 cups broccoli florets
- 1 red bell pepper, sliced
- 1 yellow bell pepper, sliced
- 3 cloves garlic, minced
- 1 tablespoon fresh ginger, minced
- 1/4 cup low-sodium soy sauce or tamari
- 2 tablespoons rice vinegar
- 1 tablespoon honey
- 1 teaspoon sesame oil
- 2 green onions, sliced
- Sesame seeds for garnish (optional)

Instructions:

1. Heat olive oil in a large skillet or wok over medium-high heat. Add chicken and cook until browned and cooked through, about 5-7 minutes. Remove chicken from skillet and set aside.
2. In the same skillet, add broccoli, bell peppers, garlic, and ginger. Sauté for 5 minutes until vegetables are tender-crisp.
3. In a small bowl, whisk together soy sauce, rice vinegar, honey, and sesame oil. Pour sauce into the skillet and stir to coat vegetables.
4. Return chicken to the skillet and toss to combine. Cook for an additional 2-3 minutes until everything is heated through.
5. Garnish with green onions and sesame seeds before serving.

Nutritional Information:

- Calories: 300
- Protein: 25g
- Carbs: 20g
- Fat: 12g

Cooking Tips:

- Serve over cauliflower rice or quinoa for a low-carb option.
- Add your favorite vegetables like snap peas or carrots for variety.

Allergen Information:

- Contains soy (soy sauce). Use coconut aminos for a soy-free option.

Sweet Potato and Black Bean Tacos

Servings: 4 | _Prep Time:_ 15 mins | _Cook Time:_ 25 mins
Ingredients:

- 2 large sweet potatoes, peeled and diced
- 2 tablespoons olive oil
- 1 teaspoon cumin
- 1 teaspoon smoked paprika
- Salt and pepper to taste
- 1 can (15 oz) black beans, drained and rinsed
- 1/4 cup red onion, finely chopped
- 1/4 cup fresh cilantro, chopped
- Juice of 1 lime
- 8 small corn tortillas
- Avocado slices, for serving

Instructions:

1. Preheat oven to 425°F (220°C). Line a baking sheet with parchment paper.
2. In a bowl, toss sweet potatoes with olive oil, cumin, smoked paprika, salt, and pepper. Spread evenly on the baking sheet.
3. Roast sweet potatoes for 20-25 minutes, or until tender and slightly crispy, stirring halfway through.
4. In a small bowl, mix black beans, red onion, cilantro, and lime juice. Season with salt and pepper.
5. Warm tortillas in a skillet or in the oven wrapped in foil.
6. To assemble tacos, divide sweet potatoes and black bean mixture among tortillas. Top with avocado slices and additional cilantro if desired.

Nutritional Information:

- Calories: 350
- Protein: 10g
- Carbs: 55g
- Fat: 12g

Cooking Tips:

- Add a dollop of Greek yogurt or a sprinkle of feta cheese for added creaminess.

- Use whole wheat tortillas for more fiber.

Allergen Information:

- Contains corn (tortillas). Use lettuce wraps for a grain-free option.

Beef and Vegetable Stew

Servings: 6 | _Prep Time:_ 20 mins | _Cook Time:_ 1 hr 30 mins
Ingredients:

- 2 tablespoons olive oil
- 1 pound beef stew meat, cubed
- Salt and pepper to taste
- 1 onion, chopped
- 3 cloves garlic, minced
- 4 cups beef broth
- 2 carrots, sliced
- 2 celery stalks, sliced
- 2 potatoes, diced
- 1 cup green beans, trimmed and cut into pieces
- 1 teaspoon dried thyme
- 1 teaspoon dried rosemary
- 2 bay leaves
- 1 tablespoon tomato paste

Instructions:

1. Heat olive oil in a large pot over medium-high heat. Season beef with salt and pepper. Brown beef in batches, removing to a plate once browned.
2. In the same pot, add onion and garlic. Sauté for 3-4 minutes until softened.
3. Return beef to the pot. Add beef broth, carrots, celery, potatoes, green beans, thyme, rosemary, bay leaves, and tomato paste. Stir to combine.
4. Bring to a boil, then reduce heat and simmer for 1-1.5 hours, or until beef is tender and vegetables are cooked through. Remove bay leaves before serving.

Nutritional Information:

- Calories: 400
- Protein: 30g
- Carbs: 35g
- Fat: 18g

Cooking Tips:

- For a thicker stew, mix 2 tablespoons cornstarch with 1/4 cup cold water and stir into the stew in the last 10 minutes of cooking.
- Serve with a side of whole-grain bread for dipping.

Allergen Information:

- None.

Cauliflower Rice with Grilled Shrimp

Servings: 4 | _Prep Time:_ 15 mins | _Cook Time:_ 10 mins
Ingredients:

- 1 head cauliflower, grated or 4 cups pre-riced cauliflower
- 1 tablespoon olive oil
- 2 cloves garlic, minced
- 1 pound large shrimp, peeled and deveined
- 1 tablespoon lemon juice
- 1 teaspoon paprika
- Salt and pepper to taste
- 2 tablespoons fresh parsley, chopped

Instructions:

1. Heat olive oil in a large skillet over medium heat. Add garlic and sauté for 1-2 minutes until fragrant.
2. Add cauliflower rice and cook, stirring frequently, for 5-7 minutes until tender. Season with salt and pepper. Transfer to a bowl and keep warm.
3. In the same skillet, add shrimp, lemon juice, paprika, salt, and pepper. Cook for 2-3 minutes on each side until shrimp are pink and opaque.
4. Serve shrimp over cauliflower rice and garnish with fresh parsley.

Nutritional Information:

- Calories: 250
- Protein: 25g
- Carbs: 12g
- Fat: 10g

Cooking Tips:

- Add a side of steamed vegetables for extra nutrients.
- Use pre-riced cauliflower for convenience.

Allergen Information:

- Contains shellfish (shrimp).

5

Snack Attack

Snacks can be a game-changer when it comes to managing PCOS. The right snacks can help maintain blood sugar balance, curb cravings, and provide a steady source of energy throughout the day. For many women with PCOS, snacking is essential for hormone regulation and avoiding the dreaded energy crashes that can lead to overeating later on.

I used to struggle with finding snacks that satisfied my hunger without spiking my blood sugar. Often, I'd reach for convenient, sugary options that only made my symptoms worse. Through trial and error, I discovered that healthy, balanced snacks could keep my blood sugar stable and help me feel more in control of my cravings and energy levels.

In this chapter, you'll find a variety of snack recipes that are easy to prepare, delicious, and specifically designed to support hormone balance and manage insulin resistance. These snacks are perfect for keeping you energized and satisfied between meals.

Mixed Nuts and Seeds Trail Mix

Servings: 10 | *Prep Time:* 5 mins | *Cook Time:* 0 mins
Ingredients:

- 1 cup almonds
- 1 cup walnuts
- 1 cup pumpkin seeds
- 1 cup sunflower seeds
- 1/2 cup dried cranberries (unsweetened)
- 1/2 cup dark chocolate chips (70% cocoa or higher)
- 1 teaspoon cinnamon

Instructions:

1. In a large bowl, combine almonds, walnuts, pumpkin seeds, sunflower seeds, dried cranberries, dark chocolate chips, and cinnamon.
2. Mix well to combine.
3. Store in an airtight container for up to two weeks.

Nutritional Information:

- Calories: 200
- Protein: 6g
- Carbs: 14g
- Fat: 15g

Cooking Tips:

- Portion out trail mix into individual servings for a convenient grab-and-go snack.
- Add a sprinkle of sea salt for a sweet and salty flavor.

Allergen Information:

- Contains nuts (almonds, walnuts). Substitute with additional seeds if needed.

Hummus and Veggie Sticks

Servings: 4 | *Prep Time:* 10 mins | *Cook Time:* 0 mins
Ingredients:

- 1 can (15 oz) chickpeas, drained and rinsed
- 2 tablespoons tahini
- 2 tablespoons olive oil
- Juice of 1 lemon
- 1 clove garlic, minced
- Salt and pepper to taste
- 1/2 teaspoon ground cumin
- 1/4 cup water
- Veggie sticks (carrots, celery, bell peppers, cucumbers) for serving

Instructions:

1. In a food processor, combine chickpeas, tahini, olive oil, lemon juice, garlic, salt, pepper, and cumin. Blend until smooth.
2. Add water as needed to achieve desired consistency.
3. Serve hummus with assorted veggie sticks.

Nutritional Information:

- Calories: 180
- Protein: 6g
- Carbs: 18g
- Fat: 10g

Cooking Tips:

- Store hummus in the refrigerator for up to a week.
- Experiment with different spices and herbs for flavor variations.

Allergen Information:

- Contains sesame (tahini).

Greek Yogurt with Honey and Almonds

Servings: 2 | *Prep Time:* 5 mins | *Cook Time:* 0 mins
Ingredients:

- 1 cup plain Greek yogurt
- 2 tablespoons honey
- 1/4 cup sliced almonds

- 1/4 teaspoon cinnamon

Instructions:

1. Divide Greek yogurt between two bowls.
2. Drizzle each serving with honey.
3. Top with sliced almonds and a sprinkle of cinnamon.

Nutritional Information:

- Calories: 250
- Protein: 15g
- Carbs: 25g
- Fat: 10g

Cooking Tips:

- Use plain Greek yogurt to avoid added sugars.
- Substitute honey with maple syrup or agave nectar if desired.

Allergen Information:

- Contains nuts (almonds). Substitute with seeds if needed.

Apple Slices with Almond Butter

Servings: 2 | *Prep Time:* 5 mins | *Cook Time:* 0 mins
Ingredients:

- 2 apples, sliced
- 4 tablespoons almond butter

Instructions:

1. Core and slice the apples.
2. Serve apple slices with almond butter for dipping.

Nutritional Information:

- Calories: 200
- Protein: 4g

- Carbs: 26g
- Fat: 10g

Cooking Tips:

- Add a sprinkle of cinnamon on the apple slices for extra flavor.
- Use different varieties of apples for a mix of sweet and tart flavors.

Allergen Information:

- Contains nuts (almond butter). Use sunflower seed butter as a substitute if needed.

Chia Seed Pudding

Servings: 4 | *Prep Time:* 10 mins | *Cook Time:* 0 mins | *Chill Time:* 2 hrs
Ingredients:

- 1/4 cup chia seeds
- 1 cup almond milk
- 1 teaspoon vanilla extract
- 2 tablespoons maple syrup
- Fresh berries for topping

Instructions:

1. In a bowl, combine chia seeds, almond milk, vanilla extract, and maple syrup. Stir well.
2. Cover and refrigerate for at least 2 hours, or overnight, until the mixture thickens to a pudding-like consistency.
3. Stir before serving and top with fresh berries.

Nutritional Information:

- Calories: 150
- Protein: 4g
- Carbs: 15g
- Fat: 8g

Cooking Tips:

- Use coconut milk for a creamier texture.
- Add a pinch of cinnamon or cocoa powder for extra flavor.

Allergen Information:

- None. Ensure almond milk is substituted with another plant-based milk if there are nut allergies.

6

Delicious Desserts

Desserts can be a tricky part of any diet, especially when managing PCOS. The good news is that you don't have to give up sweets entirely. With the right ingredients and a bit of creativity, you can enjoy delicious, satisfying desserts that won't disrupt your hormone balance or blood sugar levels.

When I first started adjusting my diet for PCOS, I struggled with intense sugar cravings. It felt like I was constantly fighting against my body. Over time, I learned that the key was not to eliminate desserts but to reinvent them. By using natural sweeteners, healthy fats, and fiber-rich ingredients, I could enjoy my favorite treats without the guilt or negative side effects.

In this chapter, you'll find a collection of dessert recipes that are both indulgent and nourishing. These recipes prioritize whole, nutrient-dense ingredients, ensuring you can satisfy your sweet tooth in a PCOS-friendly way. Remember, moderation is key, and enjoying a balanced dessert can be a wonderful part of your overall wellness journey.

Dark Chocolate Avocado Mousse

Servings: 4 | *Prep Time:* 10 mins | *Cook Time:* 0 mins
Ingredients:

- 2 ripe avocados
- 1/4 cup cocoa powder
- 1/4 cup maple syrup
- 1/4 cup almond milk
- 1 teaspoon vanilla extract
- Pinch of sea salt
- Fresh berries for topping (optional)

Instructions:

1. In a food processor, blend avocados until smooth.
2. Add cocoa powder, maple syrup, almond milk, vanilla extract, and sea salt. Blend until creamy and well combined.
3. Spoon the mousse into serving dishes and chill for at least 30 minutes before serving.
4. Top with fresh berries if desired.

Nutritional Information:

- Calories: 200
- Protein: 3g
- Carbs: 25g
- Fat: 15g

Cooking Tips:

- Use high-quality cocoa powder for the best flavor.
- Add a tablespoon of melted dark chocolate for a richer taste.

Allergen Information:

- Contains nuts (almond milk). Substitute with another plant-based milk if needed.

Coconut Flour Brownies

Servings: 12 | *Prep Time:* 15 mins | *Cook Time:* 25 mins
Ingredients:

- 1/2 cup coconut flour
- 1/2 cup cocoa powder
- 1/4 teaspoon salt
- 1/2 teaspoon baking soda
- 3 eggs
- 1/2 cup coconut oil, melted
- 1/2 cup maple syrup
- 1 teaspoon vanilla extract
- 1/2 cup dark chocolate chips

Instructions:

1. Preheat oven to 350°F (175°C). Grease an 8x8-inch baking dish or line with parchment paper.
2. In a large bowl, whisk together coconut flour, cocoa powder, salt, and baking soda.
3. In another bowl, beat eggs, melted coconut oil, maple syrup, and vanilla extract until well combined.
4. Add wet ingredients to dry ingredients and mix until smooth.
5. Stir in dark chocolate chips.
6. Pour batter into the prepared baking dish and spread evenly.
7. Bake for 20-25 minutes, or until a toothpick inserted into the center comes out clean.
8. Let cool completely before cutting into squares.

Nutritional Information:

- Calories: 180
- Protein: 4g
- Carbs: 18g
- Fat: 12g

Cooking Tips:

- Store brownies in the refrigerator for a firmer texture.
- Add a sprinkle of sea salt on top before baking for a sweet and salty treat.

Allergen Information:

- Contains eggs and coconut.

Baked Apples with Cinnamon and Walnuts

Servings: 4 | *Prep Time:* 10 mins | *Cook Time:* 30 mins

Ingredients:

- 4 apples, cored
- 1/4 cup walnuts, chopped
- 2 tablespoons coconut sugar
- 1 teaspoon cinnamon
- 1/4 teaspoon nutmeg
- 2 tablespoons coconut oil, melted
- 1/2 cup water

Instructions:

1. Preheat oven to 375°F (190°C).
2. In a small bowl, mix chopped walnuts, coconut sugar, cinnamon, nutmeg, and melted coconut oil.
3. Place cored apples in a baking dish and fill the centers with the walnut mixture.
4. Pour water into the bottom of the baking dish.
5. Bake for 25-30 minutes, or until apples are tender and filling is golden brown.

Nutritional Information:

- Calories: 150
- Protein: 2g
- Carbs: 25g
- Fat: 8g

Cooking Tips:

- Serve with a dollop of Greek yogurt for added protein.
- Use different varieties of apples for a mix of flavors.

Allergen Information:

- Contains nuts (walnuts). Substitute with seeds if needed.

Chia Seed Pudding with Berries

Servings: 4 | *Prep Time:* 10 mins | *Cook Time:* 0 mins | *Chill Time:* 2 hrs
Ingredients:

- 1/4 cup chia seeds
- 1 cup almond milk
- 1 teaspoon vanilla extract
- 2 tablespoons maple syrup
- Fresh berries for topping

Instructions:

1. In a bowl, combine chia seeds, almond milk, vanilla extract, and maple syrup. Stir well.
2. Cover and refrigerate for at least 2 hours, or overnight, until the mixture thickens to a pudding-like consistency.
3. Stir before serving and top with fresh berries.

Nutritional Information:

- Calories: 150
- Protein: 4g
- Carbs: 15g
- Fat: 8g

Cooking Tips:

- Use coconut milk for a creamier texture.
- Add a pinch of cinnamon or cocoa powder for extra flavor.

Allergen Information:

- None. Ensure almond milk is substituted with another plant-based milk if there are nut allergies.

Almond Flour Cookies

Servings: 12 | *Prep Time:* 10 mins | *Cook Time:* 12 mins
Ingredients:

- 2 cups almond flour
- 1/4 teaspoon salt
- 1/4 teaspoon baking soda
- 1/4 cup coconut oil, melted
- 1/4 cup maple syrup
- 1 teaspoon vanilla extract
- 1/2 cup dark chocolate chips

Instructions:

1. Preheat oven to 350°F (175°C). Line a baking sheet with parchment paper.
2. In a large bowl, combine almond flour, salt, and baking soda.
3. In another bowl, mix melted coconut oil, maple syrup, and vanilla extract.
4. Add wet ingredients to dry ingredients and mix until a dough forms.
5. Fold in dark chocolate chips.
6. Drop tablespoon-sized balls of dough onto the prepared baking sheet and flatten slightly.
7. Bake for 10-12 minutes, or until edges are golden brown.
8. Let cool on the baking sheet for 5 minutes before transferring to a wire rack to cool completely.

Nutritional Information:

- Calories: 160
- Protein: 4g
- Carbs: 12g
- Fat: 12g

Cooking Tips:

- Store cookies in an airtight container at room temperature for up to a week.
- Add a pinch of sea salt on top before baking for a sweet and salty treat.

Allergen Information:

- Contains nuts (almond flour, coconut oil).

7

Hormone-Healthy Beverages

Hydration is essential for overall health, but for women with PCOS, the right beverages can make a significant difference in managing symptoms and supporting hormone balance. Choosing hormone-friendly drinks can help regulate blood sugar levels, reduce inflammation, and provide essential nutrients.

I vividly recall the transformation in my energy levels and mood when I started paying attention to what I drank. Instead of reaching for sugary sodas and caffeinated beverages, I began experimenting with herbal teas, infused waters, and nutrient-rich smoothies. The changes were remarkable – I felt more energized, experienced fewer cravings, and noticed a positive shift in my overall well-being.

In this chapter, you'll find a variety of beverage recipes that are not only delicious but also beneficial for hormone balance and insulin resistance. These drinks are easy to prepare and incorporate into your daily routine, making hydration an enjoyable and health-boosting part of your day.

Herbal Teas for Hormone Balance

Servings: 4 | *Prep Time:* 5 mins | *Cook Time:* 10 mins
Ingredients:

- 4 cups water
- 2 tablespoons dried chamomile flowers
- 1 tablespoon dried raspberry leaf
- 1 tablespoon dried nettle leaf
- 1 tablespoon dried peppermint leaf
- 1 tablespoon dried lemon balm
- Honey or lemon (optional)

Instructions:

1. In a medium pot, bring water to a boil.
2. Add chamomile, raspberry leaf, nettle leaf, peppermint, and lemon balm. Reduce heat and simmer for 10 minutes.
3. Strain the tea into a teapot or large jar.
4. Sweeten with honey or lemon if desired.

Nutritional Information:

- Calories: 0 (without honey)
- Protein: 0g
- Carbs: 0g
- Fat: 0g

Cooking Tips:

- Prepare a large batch and store in the refrigerator for up to a week.
- Drink 1-2 cups daily to support hormone balance.

Allergen Information:

- None.

Green Smoothies for Insulin Resistance

Servings: 2 | _Prep Time:_ 10 mins | _Cook Time:_ 0 mins
Ingredients:

- 1 cup spinach
- 1 cup kale
- 1/2 avocado
- 1 green apple, cored and chopped
- 1 small cucumber, chopped
- 1 tablespoon chia seeds
- 1 cup unsweetened almond milk
- Juice of 1/2 lemon

Instructions:

1. In a blender, combine spinach, kale, avocado, green apple, cucumber, chia seeds, almond milk, and lemon juice.
2. Blend until smooth and creamy.
3. Pour into glasses and serve immediately.

Nutritional Information:

- Calories: 150
- Protein: 4g
- Carbs: 20g
- Fat: 7g

Cooking Tips:

- Add a scoop of protein powder for an extra protein boost.
- Use frozen greens for a colder, thicker smoothie.

Allergen Information:

- Contains nuts (almond milk). Substitute with another plant-based milk if needed.

Golden Milk with Turmeric and Ginger

Servings: 2 | _Prep Time:_ 5 mins | _Cook Time:_ 5 mins
Ingredients:

- 2 cups unsweetened coconut milk
- 1 teaspoon ground turmeric
- 1/2 teaspoon ground ginger
- 1/4 teaspoon ground cinnamon
- Pinch of black pepper
- 1 tablespoon honey or maple syrup (optional)

Instructions:

1. In a small saucepan, combine coconut milk, turmeric, ginger, cinnamon, and black pepper.
2. Heat over medium heat, whisking frequently, until hot but not boiling.
3. Remove from heat and stir in honey or maple syrup if using.
4. Pour into mugs and serve warm.

Nutritional Information:

- Calories: 100
- Protein: 1g
- Carbs: 10g
- Fat: 7g

Cooking Tips:

- Use fresh turmeric and ginger for a more potent flavor.
- Drink in the evening for a calming and anti-inflammatory effect.

Allergen Information:

- None.

Infused Water with Lemon and Mint

Servings: 4 | _Prep Time:_ 5 mins | _Cook Time:_ 0 mins
Ingredients:

- 1 lemon, thinly sliced
- 1/2 cup fresh mint leaves
- 4 cups water

Instructions:

1. In a large pitcher, combine lemon slices and mint leaves.
2. Fill the pitcher with water.
3. Refrigerate for at least 1 hour before serving.

Nutritional Information:

- Calories: 0
- Protein: 0g
- Carbs: 0g
- Fat: 0g

Cooking Tips:

- Add cucumber slices or berries for additional flavor.
- Refill the pitcher with water throughout the day as needed.

Allergen Information:

- None.

Bone Broth for Gut Health

Servings: 8 | _Prep Time:_ 10 mins | _Cook Time:_ 24 hrs
Ingredients:

- 4 pounds beef or chicken bones
- 2 tablespoons apple cider vinegar
- 1 onion, quartered
- 2 carrots, chopped
- 2 celery stalks, chopped
- 4 cloves garlic, smashed
- 10 cups water
- Salt and pepper to taste

Instructions:

1. Place bones in a large stockpot or slow cooker. Add apple cider vinegar and water, letting it sit for 30 minutes to help extract minerals from the bones.
2. Add onion, carrots, celery, and garlic.
3. Bring to a boil, then reduce to a simmer. Cook for 24 hours, skimming any foam that rises to the top.
4. Strain the broth through a fine-mesh sieve into a large bowl. Season with salt and pepper.
5. Store in the refrigerator for up to 5 days or freeze for later use.

Nutritional Information:

- Calories: 50
- Protein: 5g
- Carbs: 2g
- Fat: 2g

Cooking Tips:

- Use a variety of bones, including marrow bones, for a richer broth.
- Drink a cup daily for gut health and inflammation reduction.

Allergen Information:

- None.

8

Meal Planning and Prep

Meal planning is an essential strategy for managing PCOS. By planning your meals ahead of time, you can ensure that you have balanced, nutrient-dense options available, reducing the likelihood of reaching for unhealthy, convenient foods. Effective meal planning can help stabilize blood sugar levels, support hormone balance, and make it easier to maintain a healthy diet.

When I started meal planning, I noticed a significant improvement in my energy levels and overall well-being. It allowed me to control portions, incorporate a variety of nutrients, and save time and stress during the week. Here are some tips to help you get started with effective meal planning:

- **Start Small:** Begin with planning just a few meals each week and gradually increase as you get more comfortable.
- **Use a Template:** Create a weekly meal planning template to organize your meals and shopping list.
- **Batch Cooking:** Prepare large batches of meals and freeze individual portions for easy grab-and-go options.
- **Keep it Simple:** Choose recipes that are easy to prepare and require minimal ingredients.
- **Stay Flexible:** Be prepared to adjust your plan as needed. Life can be unpredictable, and it's okay to swap meals or make changes.

Sample Meal Plans

7-Day Meal Plan for Insulin Resistance

Day	Breakfast	Lunch	Dinner	Snack
Monday	Hormone-Balancing Smoothie Bowl	Quinoa and Black Bean Salad	Baked Salmon with Asparagus	Apple Slices with Almond Butter
Tuesday	Insulin-Resistant-Friendly Oatmeal	Grilled Chicken and Veggie Wraps	Chicken Stir-Fry with Broccoli	Mixed Nuts and Seeds Trail Mix
Wednesday	Egg Muffins with Veggies	Lentil and Spinach Soup	Sweet Potato and Black Bean Tacos	Greek Yogurt with Honey and Almonds

Day	Breakfast	Lunch	Dinner	Snack
Thursday	Greek Yogurt Parfaits	Tuna and Avocado Salad	Beef and Vegetable Stew	Hummus and Veggie Sticks
Friday	Avocado and Smoked Salmon Toast	Zucchini Noodles with Pesto	Cauliflower Rice with Grilled Shrimp	Chia Seed Pudding
Saturday	Hormone-Balancing Smoothie Bowl	Quinoa and Black Bean Salad	Baked Salmon with Asparagus	Apple Slices with Almond Butter
Sunday	Insulin-Resistant-Friendly Oatmeal	Grilled Chicken and Veggie Wraps	Chicken Stir-Fry with Broccoli	Mixed Nuts and Seeds Trail Mix

7-Day Meal Plan for Hormone Balance

Day	Breakfast	Lunch	Dinner	Snack
Monday	Avocado and Smoked Salmon Toast	Quinoa and Black Bean Salad	Baked Salmon with Asparagus	Greek Yogurt with Honey and Almonds
Tuesday	Insulin-Resistant-Friendly Oatmeal	Grilled Chicken and Veggie Wraps	Chicken Stir-Fry with Broccoli	Hummus and Veggie Sticks
Wednesday	Egg Muffins with Veggies	Lentil and Spinach Soup	Sweet Potato and Black Bean Tacos	Chia Seed Pudding
Thursday	Greek Yogurt Parfaits	Tuna and Avocado Salad	Beef and Vegetable Stew	Mixed Nuts and Seeds Trail Mix
Friday	Hormone-Balancing Smoothie Bowl	Zucchini Noodles with Pesto	Cauliflower Rice with Grilled Shrimp	Apple Slices with Almond Butter
Saturday	Insulin-Resistant-Friendly Oatmeal	Quinoa and Black Bean Salad	Baked Salmon with Asparagus	Greek Yogurt with Honey and Almonds
Sunday	Avocado and Smoked Salmon Toast	Grilled Chicken and Veggie Wraps	Chicken Stir-Fry with Broccoli	Hummus and Veggie Sticks

These meal plans provide a structured guide to help you manage insulin resistance and balance hormones with nutrient-dense, delicious meals. Each plan incorporates a variety of breakfasts, lunches, dinners, and snacks to keep your diet diverse and enjoyable. Remember to stay flexible and adjust the plans according to your personal preferences and needs.

9

Tips and Techniques

Cooking Tips for PCOS-Friendly Meals

1. **Ingredient Substitutions and Swaps**

   ◦ **Refined Carbs:** Swap white rice and pasta for whole grains like quinoa, brown rice, or whole wheat pasta.
   ◦ **Sugars:** Replace refined sugar with natural sweeteners like honey, maple syrup, or stevia.
   ◦ **Flour:** Use almond flour, coconut flour, or oat flour instead of all-purpose flour.
   ◦ **Dairy:** Substitute cow's milk with plant-based milks like almond, coconut, or oat milk.
   ◦ **Oils:** Use healthy fats like olive oil, avocado oil, or coconut oil instead of vegetable or canola oil.

2. **Tips for Reducing Sugar and Refined Carbs**

   ◦ **Read Labels:** Be mindful of hidden sugars in packaged foods. Look for terms like high fructose corn syrup, cane sugar, and glucose.
   ◦ **Cook at Home:** Preparing meals at home gives you control over ingredients and allows you to reduce added sugars and refined carbs.
   ◦ **Focus on Whole Foods:** Incorporate more vegetables, fruits, lean proteins, and whole grains into your diet.
   ◦ **Use Spices and Herbs:** Enhance the flavor of your dishes with natural spices and herbs instead of relying on sugary sauces or dressings.
   ◦ **Plan Your Meals:** Create a weekly meal plan to ensure you're incorporating balanced meals that minimize refined carbs and sugars.

3. **Techniques for Adding More Fiber and Protein to Meals**

- **Fiber:** Add chia seeds, flaxseeds, or psyllium husk to smoothies, yogurt, or oatmeal for a fiber boost.
- **Protein:** Include a source of protein in every meal, such as eggs, chicken, fish, legumes, or tofu.
- **Vegetables:** Increase your intake of fiber-rich vegetables like broccoli, Brussels sprouts, and leafy greens.
- **Beans and Legumes:** Incorporate beans, lentils, and chickpeas into soups, stews, and salads.
- **Nuts and Seeds:** Snack on nuts and seeds or add them to salads, yogurt, and oatmeal for added fiber and protein.

Shopping Guide

1. **Essential Pantry Staples for PCOS-Friendly Cooking**

   - **Grains:** Quinoa, brown rice, whole wheat pasta, oats
   - **Flours:** Almond flour, coconut flour, oat flour
   - **Sweeteners:** Honey, maple syrup, stevia
   - **Oils:** Olive oil, avocado oil, coconut oil
   - **Proteins:** Canned beans, lentils, chickpeas, nuts, seeds
   - **Spices and Herbs:** Cinnamon, turmeric, ginger, garlic, basil, cilantro
   - **Plant-Based Milks:** Almond milk, coconut milk, oat milk
   - **Canned Goods:** Diced tomatoes, coconut milk, vegetable broth
   - **Nut Butters:** Almond butter, sunflower seed butter, peanut butter (in moderation)

2. **Tips for Grocery Shopping on a Budget**

   - **Plan Your Meals:** Create a weekly meal plan and shopping list to avoid impulse buys and ensure you have all necessary ingredients.
   - **Buy in Bulk:** Purchase staples like grains, beans, and nuts in bulk to save money.
   - **Seasonal Produce:** Choose fruits and vegetables that are in season for better prices and freshness.
   - **Frozen Fruits and Vegetables:** Stock up on frozen produce, which is often cheaper and just as nutritious as fresh.
   - **Store Brands:** Opt for store-brand products, which are typically less expensive than name brands.

- **Coupons and Discounts:** Take advantage of coupons, sales, and discounts to save on groceries.
- **Farmer's Markets:** Shop at farmer's markets for fresh, locally sourced produce that can be more affordable.

As we reach the end of "Meals She Eats: A PCOS Cookbook for Insulin Resistance Diet, Hormone Balance, and Period Repair Manual," I want to leave you with some final thoughts and encouragement. Managing PCOS is a journey that requires patience, persistence, and self-compassion. The road may have its ups and downs, but with the right tools and mindset, you can make significant strides towards better health.

Remember, each meal is an opportunity to nourish your body and support your well-being. The recipes in this cookbook are designed to help you enjoy delicious, satisfying meals while managing your symptoms and promoting hormone balance. Embrace the process, experiment with new ingredients, and have fun in the kitchen. Your health journey is unique, and every small step you take is a victory.

Thank you for allowing me to be a part of your journey. I hope these recipes bring you joy, comfort, and improved health. Stay motivated, stay positive, and remember that you have the power to make choices that benefit your health every day. Wishing you all the best on your path to wellness.

Resources and Further Reading

To further support your journey with PCOS, here are some recommended books, websites, and resources:

1. **Books:**

    ○ "The PCOS Plan: Prevent and Reverse Polycystic Ovary Syndrome through Diet and Fasting" by Dr. Jason Fung and Nadia Brito Pateguana
    ○ "8 Steps to Reverse Your PCOS: A Proven Program to Reset Your Hormones, Repair Your Metabolism, and Restore Your Fertility" by Fiona McCulloch, ND
    ○ "PCOS SOS: A Gynecologist's Lifeline To Naturally Restore Your Rhythms, Hormones, and Happiness" by Dr. Felice Gersh

2. **Websites:**

    ○ PCOS Challenge: A comprehensive resource for PCOS information, support, and advocacy.

- The PCOS Nutrition Center: Offers nutrition advice, recipes, and resources for managing PCOS.
- Hormone Health Network: Provides educational materials and resources on hormone-related conditions, including PCOS.

3. **Support Groups:**

- Join online support groups and forums such as the PCOS Challenge Support Group on Facebook or Reddit's r/PCOS community to connect with others who share similar experiences and challenges.

4. **Healthcare Providers:**

- Work with a healthcare provider who specializes in PCOS to develop a personalized plan for managing your symptoms. This could include a registered dietitian, endocrinologist, or naturopathic doctor.

Creating this cookbook has been a labor of love, and it wouldn't have been possible without the support and contributions of many wonderful individuals. I would like to extend my deepest gratitude to:

- **My Family and Friends:** Your unwavering support and encouragement have been my rock throughout this journey. Thank you for believing in me and for your endless taste-testing.
- **Healthcare Professionals:** Thank you to the doctors, dietitians, and researchers who have dedicated their careers to understanding and treating PCOS. Your work is invaluable.
- **Recipe Testers:** A heartfelt thank you to all the amazing individuals who tested these recipes and provided invaluable feedback. Your input has made this cookbook even better.
- **Readers and Followers:** To everyone who has followed my journey and supported my work, thank you. Your stories, feedback, and enthusiasm inspire me every day.
- **Design and Publishing Team:** Thank you to the talented designers, editors, and publishers who brought this cookbook to life. Your expertise and creativity have been instrumental.

Thank you once again for joining me on this journey. I hope "Meals She Eats" becomes a cherished resource in your kitchen and a valuable tool in your journey towards better health.

Wishing you wellness and happiness,

Lila Thompson.

Made in United States
Troutdale, OR
12/20/2024

26966559R00053